C29 0000 0866 727

D1380084

First published in Great Britain 2023 by Red Shed,
part of Farshore

An imprint of HarperCollins*Publishers*
1 London Bridge Street
London SE1 9GF
www.farshore.co.uk

HarperCollins*Publishers*
Macken House, 39/40 Mayor Street Upper,
Dublin 1, D01 C9W8, Ireland

Text and illustrations copyright © Sophy Henn 2023
Sophy Henn has asserted her moral rights.

ISBN 978-0-00-853430-1
Printed in Italy.
001

Consultancy by Paul Lawston.

A CIP catalogue record for this book is available
from the British Library.

All rights reserved. No part of this publication may be
reproduced, stored in a retrieval system, or transmitted,
in any form or by any means, electronic, mechanical,
photocopying, recording or otherwise, without the
prior permission of the publisher and copyright owner.

Stay safe online. Farshore is not responsible for
content hosted by third parties.

Farshore takes its responsibility to the planet and
its inhabitants very seriously. We aim to use papers
from well-managed forests run by responsible suppliers.

LIFESIZE

Sophy Henn

DEADLY ANIMALS

Here are the **LIFESIZE** deadly talons of the harpy eagle, the most powerful eagle in the world. The harpy has the largest talons of any eagle and they are also bigger than a grizzly bear's! LOOK OUT!

RED SHED

Are you feeling brave? Yes? Then welcome to *LIFESIZE DEADLY ANIMALS*, which is packed with some of the deadliest creatures on the planet, from the dangerously small to the lethally MASSIVE. But just how small and massive are they?

Well, you can see for yourself because every time you see the word **LIFESIZE** in this book, you will know you are looking at an animal, or a bit of an animal, that is actual size!

So let's go on a **LIFESIZE** deadly animal adventure, meeting the extremely venomous and the utterly ferocious, and see how you, and your family, measure up against them . . .

Here's a **LIFESIZE** cheetah paw – they are one of the reasons why cheetahs are such successful predators. When they run, their claws stick into the ground. This helps them reach incredible speeds to catch their prey.

The cheetah is SUPER fast but it isn't the MOST successful predator. Can you guess what that is? Let's see if you're right . . .

. . . it's the DRAGONFLY!

I bet you didn't guess that! However, dragonflies like these **LIFESIZE** ones here are nearly twice as successful at catching their prey than cheetahs. They triumph nine times out of ten!

But how?

Well, along with being able to fly **SUPER FAST**, dragonflies can fly forwards, backwards, up, down and even upside down! This is all ever so useful when they are chasing small insects.

Look! A **LIFESIZE** roseate skimmer. Like all dragonflies, the females actually lay their eggs when they are flying.

This is a **LIFESIZE** giant darner. All dragonflies are carnivores (meat eaters). When they are young (nymphs) they eat insects and even tadpoles and small fish, but adults eat only insects.

Dragonflies also have AMAZING eyesight, thanks to their two huge eyes that almost cover their whole head. Both of these eyes are made up of about 30,000 tiny eyes! All these eyes give them an almost 360-degree view, so they can see their prey easily.

Here is a **LIFESIZE** flame skimmer. Like many dragonflies, the males have flying contests to win the best spot to perch for the day.

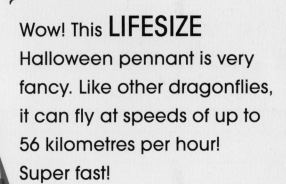

Wow! This **LIFESIZE** Halloween pennant is very fancy. Like other dragonflies, it can fly at speeds of up to 56 kilometres per hour! Super fast!

AND dragonflies have special, super speedy neurons (which are like little messengers in the brain) that help them spot when their prey has changed direction and send a lightning-fast message to their wings to change direction too.

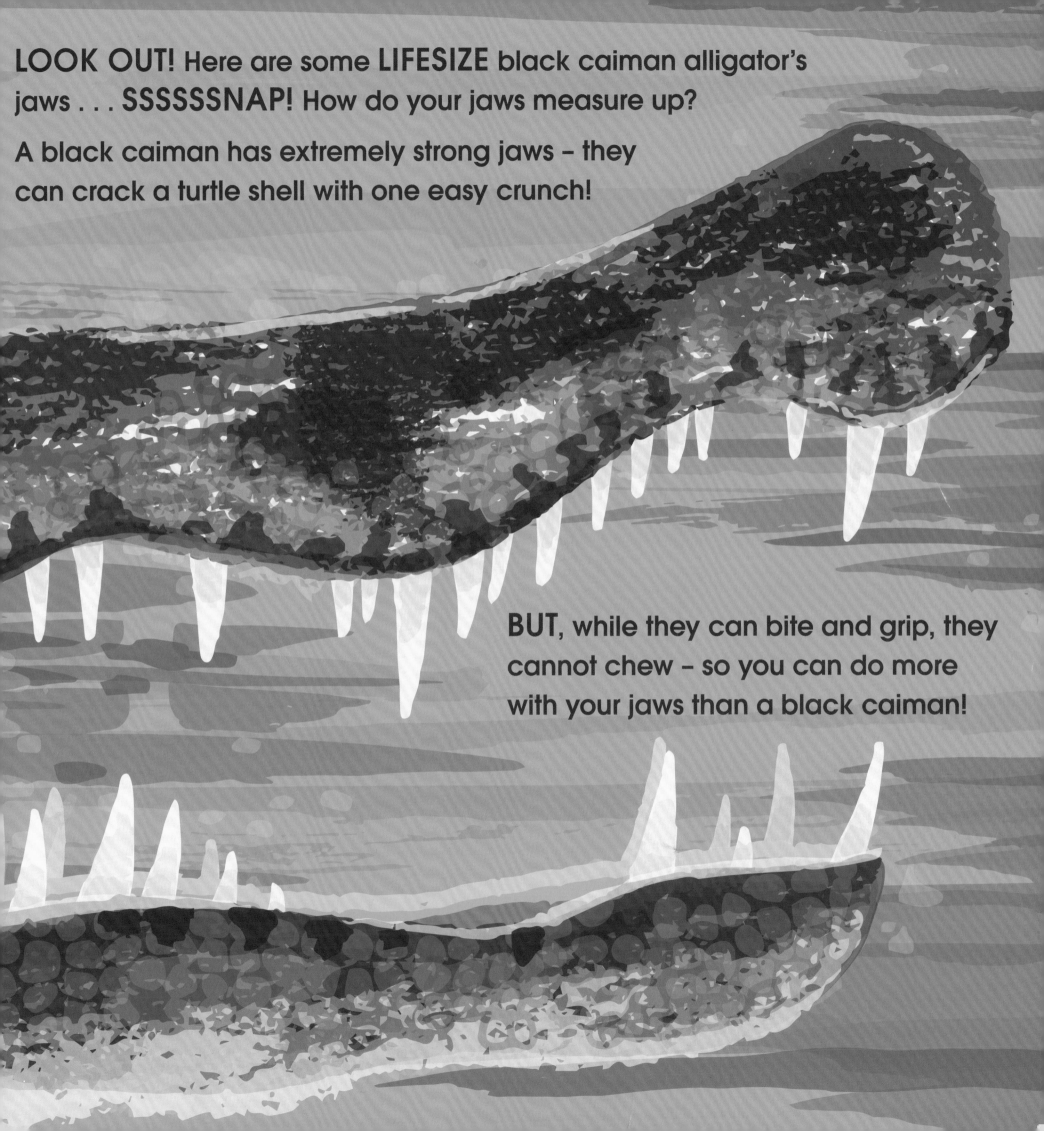

LOOK OUT! Here are some **LIFESIZE** black caiman alligator's jaws . . . **SSSSSSNAP!** How do your jaws measure up?

A black caiman has extremely strong jaws – they can crack a turtle shell with one easy crunch!

BUT, while they can bite and grip, they cannot chew – so you can do more with your jaws than a black caiman!

The **black caiman** lives in the Amazon rainforest. In fact, it is the largest apex predator that lives here. Apex means it is at the top of its food chain with no other animal trying to eat it!

But what other deadly creatures live here?

The electric eel gives off two super fast electric pulses if it thinks there might be prey nearby. These pulses make the prey twitch so the eel can spot and catch it. Then the eel shocks it with up to 400 high-voltage pulses per second, paralyzing the prey so the eel can eat it.

Here are some **LIFESIZE** bullet ants. They have the most painful and potent sting of any insect, which can leave you in agony for up to a whole day and night!

WOW! Look at these **LIFESIZE** blue poison dart frogs. They are blue to warn predators not to eat them as they are extremely poisonous, but these frogs are only poisonous because they eat extremely poisonous bugs. If these frogs didn't eat them, they wouldn't be poisonous anymore!

This **LIFESIZE** Bengal slow loris is cute but it is also DEADLY . . . in fact, slow lorises are the only venomous primates we know of. To produce their deadly, flesh-rotting venom, they mix oil from a sweat gland in their armpit with their saliva. But don't worry, they only seem to use their venom on each other!

Can you lick your own armpit?

Bengal slow lorises live in China (and also southeast Asia) and tend to be nocturnal, which means they are awake at night and sleep during the day.

What other deadly animals are up at night in China?

Malayan porcupines aren't exactly deadly, but they defend themselves from predators with their incredible quills. The quills are actually super-strong hairs, which stick into anything that attacks the porcupines. OUCH!

The South China tiger is a stealthy hunter. It sneaks up on its prey and then pounces. Tigers have the biggest canine teeth of all the wild cats, growing up to 7.6 centimetres long.

Here is a LIFESIZE Chinese bird spider and just one bite could leave you unable to move. But it is sneaky and usually hides in a burrow until its prey comes close, then . . . SURPRISE!

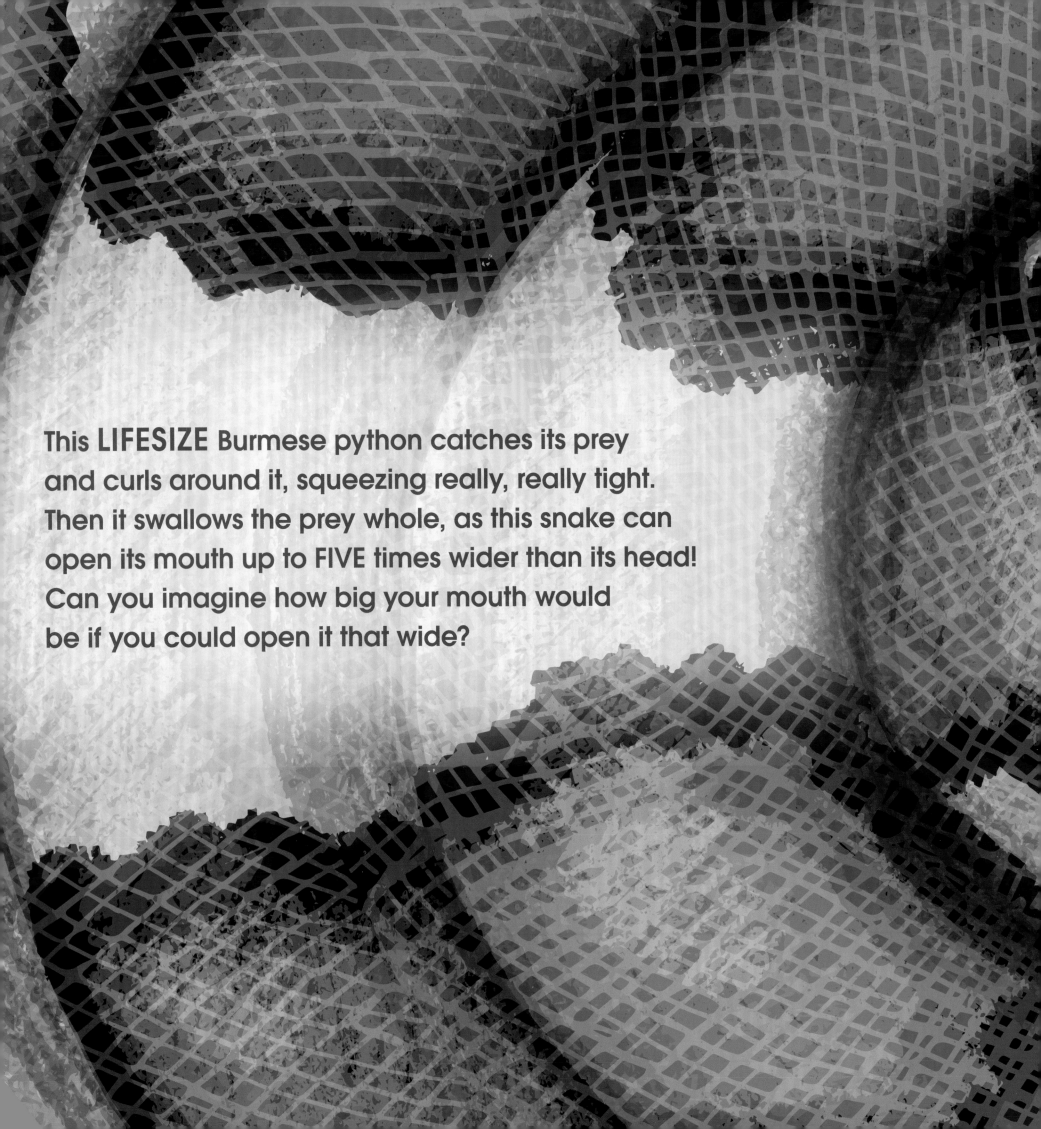

This **LIFESIZE** Burmese python catches its prey
and curls around it, squeezing really, really tight.
Then it swallows the prey whole, as this snake can
open its mouth up to **FIVE** times wider than its head!
Can you imagine how big your mouth would
be if you could open it that wide?

Burmese pythons live in the jungles of southeast Asia and Florida, USA. Here, in this Thai jungle, they live alongside these other deadly animals . . .

Clouded leopards have the largest teeth, in relation to their size, of any wild cat. They use these teeth when hunting their prey. They mainly hunt on the ground but are also brilliant climbers and can hang from tree branches upside down!

When Burmese pythons are young they live up in trees, but when they are fully-grown they are too big and heavy for the branches, so have to stay on the ground or in the water. Luckily they are excellent swimmers!

Even though a Malayan sun bear has fearsome teeth and claws, it's actually its super-long tongue that it uses the most when hunting for food. A sun bear's tongue can grow up to 25 centimetres long and the bear uses it to scoop out termites and honey from trees and bees' nests.

Like the Burmese python, this LIFESIZE Vietnamese centipede curls around its prey, such as mice or small lizards. However, instead of squeezing them, it uses special legs near its head to inject them with deadly venom. OUCH!

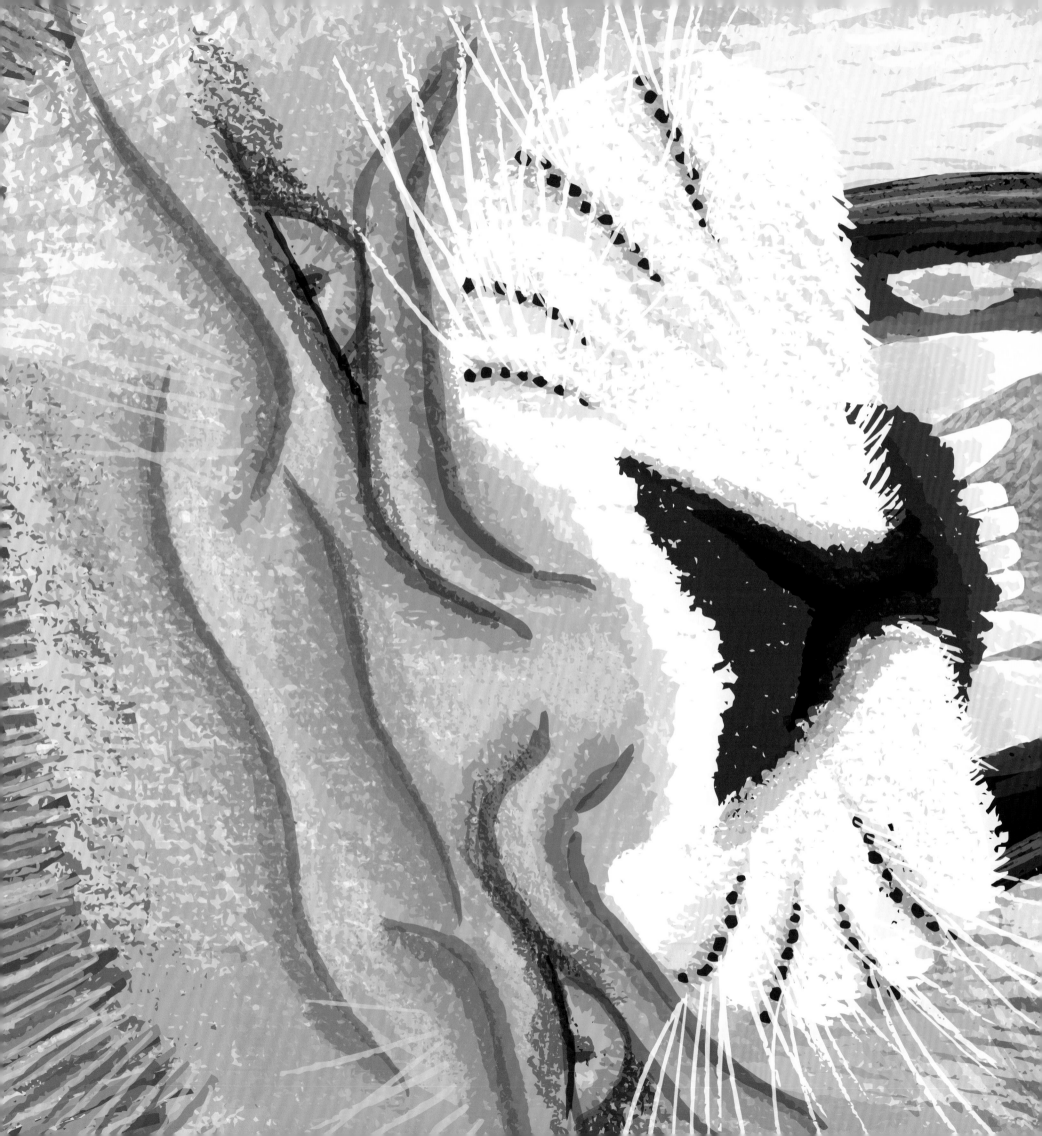

Here is a lion's LIFESIZE ferocious tongue.

YES, TONGUE! A lion's tongue is covered
with tiny spines that face backwards, and with
just a lick or two, a lion could remove all the skin
from the back of your hand . . . OWWWWW!

Is your tongue as long as this lion's?

By a watering hole in the savannah of Africa, this **lion** is eating its prey using its three different kinds of teeth. One type for gripping, one for tearing and one for cutting.

What other deadly animals live here?

This **LIFESIZE** giant deathstalker scorpion uses its deadly venom in two ways. It can inject the venom into its prey to kill it OR spray the venom into an attacker's eyes to paralyze it so the scorpion can then make a quick getaway.

Painted wolves enjoy a joyful greeting ceremony before they all go out to hunt. When they are hunting the wolves work together and even talk to each other using barks and howls. This makes them very successful hunters, catching their prey eight times out of ten!

These hippos might look cute and cuddly, but they are the deadliest land mammal on the planet and have the strongest bite of any mammal. They can also run pretty fast, reaching speeds of up to 48 kilometres per hour.

This black-footed cat is the smallest wild cat in Africa and also the deadliest! It is almost three times more successful at hunting than a lion!

Great white sharks can get through thousands of teeth in their lifetime! They lose their teeth often but if one falls out another moves in to replace it. While great whites live in lots of oceans, this one lives in the Indo-Pacific, near Australia.

But what other deadly creatures live here?

A spotted porcupinefish has enough poison in it to kill 30 adult humans, but it is only poisonous when eaten.

If a spotted porcupinefish is in danger, it can puff itself up to over twice its original size and its spines will stick out. This shows predators that it would make a very painful, or even deadly, snack!

Australian box jellyfish are considered to be the most venomous sea animal, with tiny poison darts all over their long, long tentacles. Unlike other jellyfish they also have eyes, which leads us to believe they hunt their prey, instead of just accidentally catching it like other jellyfish.

This **LIFESIZE** geographic cone snail delivers its venom via a spearlike tooth that shoots out and paralyzes its fishy prey instantly. This means the fish can't swim away and leave the cone snail without its dinner.

6.5 LIFESIZE books

Harpy eagle
Wingspan:
up to 2 metres

Did you know? Harpy eagles' legs and talons are so strong they can crush bones.

WOW! We have travelled all over the world and seen some astonishing **LIFESIZE** deadly animals. Let's see how they compare in size to each other . . .

Black caiman
Head to tail:
up to 4.5 metres

Did you know? Black caimans can use their powerful jaws to crush or drown their prey by holding it underwater.

15 LIFESIZE books

Burmese python
Head to tail:
up to 7 metres

Did you know? Burmese pythons are excellent swimmers and can stay underwater for up to 30 minutes.

23 LIFESIZE books

Great white shark

Head to tail:
up to 6 metres

Did you know? Great white sharks can detect blood up to 400 metres away.

20 LIFESIZE books

Roseate skimmer dragonfly

Wingspan:
up to 8.5 centimetres

Did you know? Dragonflies have been around since before the dinosaurs (over 300 million years!).

But where do you fit into this deadly line-up? Measure yourself using this book to find out. You could even measure your friends and family to see where they fit in!

Bengal slow loris

Head to tail:
up to 37 centimetres

Did you know? Slow lorises have incredible eyesight and can see in almost total darkness.

1 LIFESIZE book

Lion

Head to tail:
up to 2.5 metres

Did you know? Lions can eat up to a quarter of their body weight in a single meal.

8 LIFESIZE books

Cheetah

Head to tail:
up to 2.2 metres

Did you know? Cheetahs can get up to a speed of 100 kilometres per hour in just three seconds.

7 LIFESIZE books